ODE

INTIMATIONS OF IMMORTALITY

FROM RECOLLECTIONS OF EARLY CHILDHOOD

BY
WILLIAM WORDSWORTH

DOVE COTTAGE, GRASMERE

BOSTON
D. LOTHROP AND COMPANY
FRANKLIN AND HAWLEY STREETS

Press of Berwick & Smith, 118 Purchase Street.

APPARELLED IN CELESTIAL LIGHT.

WILLIAM WORDSWORTH.

[*Photographed from the painting by Mr. Henry Inman
(1844), now in possession of Mrs. Reed,
Philadelphia, Pa.*]

WILLIAM WORDSWORTH.

[*Photographed from a portrait on ivory, painted in* 1841 *by
Miss Margaret Gillies, and now in possession of
Mr. William Wordsworth.*]

AUTHOR'S NOTE.

This was composed during my residence at Town-end, Grasmere. Two years at least passed between the writing of the four first stanzas and the remaining part. To the attentive and competent reader the whole sufficiently explains itself; but there may be no harm in adverting here to particular feelings or *experiences* of my own mind on which the structure of the poem partly rests. Nothing was more difficult for me in childhood than to admit the notion of death as a state applicable to my own being. I have said elsewhere,

> " A simple child,
> That lightly draws its breath,
> And feels its life in every limb,
> What should it know of death ! "

But it was not so much from feelings of animal vivacity that my difficulty came as from a sense of the indomitableness of the spirit within me. I used to brood over the stories of Enoch and Elijah, and almost to persuade myself that, whatever might become of others, I should be translated, in something of the same way, to heaven. With a feeling congenial to this, I was often unable to think of external things as having external existence, and I communed with all that I saw as something not apart from, but inherent in, my own immaterial nature. Many times while going to school have I grasped at a wall or tree to recall myself from this abyss of idealism to the reality. At that time I was afraid of such processes. In later periods of life I have deplored, as we have all reason to do, a subjugation of an opposite character, and have rejoiced over the remembrances, as is expressed in the lines,

> "Obstinate questionings
> Of sense and outward things,
> Fallings from us, vanishings."

To that dream-like vividness and splendor which invest objects of sight in childhood, every one, I believe, if he would look back, could bear testimony, and I need not dwell upon it here; but having in the poem regarded it as presumptive evidence of a prior state of existence, I think it right to protest against a conclusion, which has given pain to some good and pious persons, that I meant to inculcate such a belief. It is far too shadowy a notion to be recommended to faith, as more than an element in our instincts of immortality. But let us bear in mind that, though the idea is not advanced in revelation, there is nothing there to contradict it, and the fall of man presents an analogy in its favor. Accordingly, a preexistent state has entered into the popular creeds of many nations; and, among all persons acquainted with classic literature, is known as an ingredient in Platonic philosophy. Archimedes said that he could move the world if he had a point whereon to rest his machine. Who has not felt the same aspirations as regards the world of his own mind? Having to wield some of its elements when I was impelled to write this poem on the "Immortality of the Soul," I took hold of the notion of pre-existence as having sufficient foundation in humanity for authorizing me to make for my purpose the best use of it I could as a poet.

ILLUSTRATIONS.

The engraving by George L. Cowee and John Schoelch.

ACKNOWLEDGMENT is due the WORDSWORTH SOCIETY (England), through whose courtesy, by its Secretary, Professor William Knight, the two portraits of Wordsworth in this volume are given. They are from a set of five photographs from the originals, prepared for the members of the Society.

It may not be amiss to quote here, from the *Transactions* of the Society (No. IV.), what is said of the Inman portrait, which, out of some twenty-seven, Mr. Wordsworth himself considered the best likeness: "The true man, Wordsworth, as he was, as he lived and moved among the sons of men . . . . speaks in the Inman picture. It is a likeness. It is the man, with the far-off gaze, who wrote the poems."

INTIMATIONS OF IMMORTALITY

FROM RECOLLECTIONS OF EARLY CHILDHOOD.

The Child is father of the Man;
And I could wish my days to be
Bound each to each by natural piety.

I.

THERE was a time when meadow, grove, and
    stream,
The earth, and every common sight,
    To me did seem
    Apparelled in celestial light,
The glory and the freshness of a dream.

It is not now as it hath been of yore;—

    Turn wheresoe'er I may,

      By night or day,

The things which I have seen I now can see no

    more.

        II.

    The Rainbow comes and goes,

    And lovely is the Rose,

    The Moon doth with delight

Look round her when the heavens are bare,

    Waters on a starry night

    Are beautiful and fair;

    The sunshine is a glorious birth;

    But yet I know, where'er I go,

That there hath passed away a glory from the

    earth.

AND WHILE THE YOUNG LAMBS BOUND
AS TO THE TABOR'S SOUND.

III.

Now, while the birds thus sing a joyous song,

And while the young lambs bound

As to the tabor's sound,

To me alone there came a thought of grief:

A timely utterance gave that thought relief,

And I again am strong:

The cataracts blow their trumpets from the steep;

No more shall grief of mine the season wrong;

I hear the Echoes through the mountains throng,

The Winds come to me from the fields of sleep,

And all the earth is gay;

Land and sea

Give themselves up to jollity,

And with the heart of May

Doth every Beast keep holiday; —

Thou Child of Joy,

Shout round me, let me hear thy shouts, thou
happy Shepherd-boy!

IV.

Ye blessèd Creatures, I have heard the call

Ye to each other make; I see

The heavens laugh with you in your jubilee ;

My heart is at your festival,

My head hath its coronal,

The fulness of your bliss, I feel — I feel it all.

Oh evil day! if I were sullen

While Earth herself is adorning,

This sweet May-morning,

And the Children are culling

On every side,

In a thousand valleys far and wide,

AND THE BABE LEAPS UP ON HIS MOTHER'S ARM.

Fresh flowers; while the sun shines warm,

And the Babe leaps up on his Mother's arm: —

I hear, I hear, with joy I hear!

— But there's a Tree, of many, one,

A single Field which I have looked upon,

Both of them speak of something that is gone:

The Pansy at my feet

Doth the same tale repeat:

Whither is fled the visionary gleam?

Where is it now, the glory and the dream?

V.

Our birth is but a sleep and a forgetting:

The soul that rises with us, our life's Star,

Hath had elsewhere its setting,

And cometh from afar:

Not in entire forgetfulness,

And not in utter nakedness,

But trailing clouds of glory do we come
        From God, who is our home:
Heaven lies about us in our infancy!
Shades of the prison-house begin to close
        Upon the growing Boy,
But he beholds the light, and whence it flows
        He sees it in his joy;
The Youth, who daily farther from the east
        Must travel, still is Nature's Priest,
        And by the vision splendid
        Is on his way attended;
At length the Man perceives it die away,
And fade into the light of common day.

                    VI.

Earth fills her lap with pleasures of her own;
Yearnings she hath in her own natural kind,

BEHOLD THE CHILD AMONG HIS NEW-BORN BLISSES,
A SIX YEARS' DARLING OF A PIGMY SIZE!

And even with something of a Mother's mind,

    And no unworthy aim,

    The homely Nurse doth all she can

To make her Foster-child, her Inmate Man,

    Forget the glories he hath known,

And that imperial palace whence he came.

VII.

Behold the Child among his new-born blisses,

A six years' Darling of a pigmy size!

See, where 'mid work of his own hand he lies,

Fretted by sallies of his mother's kisses,

With light upon him from his father's eyes!

See, at his feet, some little plan or chart,

Some fragment from his dream of human life,

Shaped by himself with newly-learned art:

A wedding or a festival,

A mourning or a funeral,

And this hath now his heart,

And unto this he frames his song,

Then will he fit his tongue

To dialogues of business, love, or strife;

But it will not be long

Ere this be thrown aside,

And with new joy and pride

The little Actor cons another part;

Filling from time to time his "humorous stage"

With all the Persons, down to palsied Age,

That Life brings with her in her equipage,

As if his whole vocation

Were endless imitation.

THOU LITTLE CHILD, YET GLORIOUS IN THE MIGHT
OF HEAVEN-BORN FREEDOM ON THY BEING'S HEIGHT.

VIII.

Thou, whose exterior semblance doth belie

Thy Soul's immensity;

Thou best Philosopher, who yet dost keep

Thy heritage, thou Eye among the blind,

That, deaf and silent, read'st the eternal deep,

Haunted forever by the eternal mind, —

Mighty prophet! Seer blest!

On whom those truths do rest,

Which we are toiling all our lives to find,

In darkness lost, the darkness of the grave;

Thou, over whom thy Immortality

Broods like the Day, a Master o'er a Slave,

A Presence which is not to be put by;

Thou little Child, yet glorious in the might

Of heaven-born freedom on thy being's height,

Why with such earnest pains dost thou provoke

The years to bring the inevitable yoke,

Thus blindly with thy blessedness at strife?

Full soon thy Soul shall have her earthly freight,

And custom lie upon thee with a weight,

Heavy as frost, and deep almost as life!

IX.

O joy! that in our embers

Is something that doth live,

That Nature yet remembers

What was so fugitive!

The thought of our past years in me doth breed

Perpetual benediction: not indeed

For that which is most worthy to be blest;

Delight and liberty, the simple creed

Of Childhood, whether busy or at rest,

With new-fledged hopes still fluttering in his breast:

THE THOUGHT OF OUR PAST YEARS IN ME DOTH
BREED PERPETUAL BENEDICTION . . . .

Not for these I raise

The song of thanks and praise;

But for those obstinate questionings

Of sense and outward things,

Fallings from us, vanishings;

Blank misgivings of a Creature

Moving about in worlds not realized,

High instincts before which our mortal Nature

Did tremble like a guilty thing surprised:

But for those first affections,

Those shadowy recollections,

Which, be they what they may,

Are yet the fountain light of all our day,

Are yet a master light of all our seeing;

Uphold us, cherish, and have power to make

Our noisy years seem moments in the being

Of the eternal Silence: truths that wake,

To perish never;

Which neither listlessness, nor mad endeavor,

Nor Man nor Boy,

Nor all that is at enmity with joy,

Can utterly abolish or destroy!

Hence in a season of calm weather,

Though inland far we be,

Our Souls have sight of that immortal sea

Which brought us hither,

Can in a moment travel thither,

And see the Children sport upon the shore,

And hear the mighty waters rolling evermore.

X.

Then sing, ye Birds, sing, sing a joyous song!

And let the young lambs bound

As to the tabor's sound!

We in thought will join your throng,

Ye that pipe and ye that play,

YE THAT PIPE AND YE THAT PLAY.

Ye that through your hearts to-day

Feel the gladness of the May!

What though the radiance which was once so bright

Be now forever taken from my sight,

Though nothing can bring back the hour

Of splendor in the grass, of glory in the flower;

We will grieve not, rather find

Strength in what remains behind;

In the primal sympathy

Which having been must ever be;

In the soothing thoughts that spring

Out of human suffering;

In the faith that looks through death

In years that bring the philosophic mind.

XI.

And O, ye Fountains, Meadows, Hills, and Groves,

Forbode not any severing of our loves!

Yet in my heart of hearts I feel your might;

I only have relinquished one delight

To live beneath your more habitual sway.

I love the Brooks which down their channels fret,

Even more than when I tripped lightly as they;

The innocent brightness of a new-born Day

Is lovely yet;

The Clouds that gather round the setting sun

Do take a sober coloring from an eye

That hath kept watch o'er man's mortality;

Another race hath been, and other palms are won.

Thanks to the human heart by which we live,

Thanks to its tenderness, its joys, and fears,

To me the meanest flower that blows can give

Thoughts that do often lie too deep for tears.

NOTES.

[From the edition of Wordsworth's Poetical Works (Edinburgh, 1883), edited by William Knight, LL.D., Secretary of the Wordsworth Society (England), and Professor of Moral Philosophy, St. Andrews, Scotland.]

THE edition of 1807 concluded with this poem, which Wordsworth simply named *Ode*, prefixing to it the motto, "Paulò majora canamus." In 1815, when he revised the poem throughout, he named it, in the characteristic manner of many of his titles — diffuse and yet precise — *Ode. Intimations of Immortality from Recollections of Early Childhood;* and he then prefixed to it the lines of his own earlier poem on the Rainbow (March, 1802):

> The child is Father of the Man;
> And I could wish my days to be
> Bound each to each by natural piety.

This longer title and motto it retained in all the subsequent editions.

The *Ode on Immortality* was written at intervals, between the years 1803 and 1806; and it was subjected to frequent and careful revision. No poem of Wordsworth's bears more evident traces in its structure at once of inspiration and elaboration; of original flight of thought and *afflatus* on the one hand, and on the other of careful sculpture and fastidious choice of phrase. But it is remarkable that there are very few changes of text in the successive editions. Most of the

alterations were made before 1815, and the omission of some
feeble lines which originally stood in stanza viii., in the
editions of 1807 and 1815, was a great advantage in disen-
cumbering the poem. The main revision and elaboration of
this Ode, however — an elaboration which suggests the passage of
the glacier ice over the rocks of White Moss Common, where
the poem was murmured out stanza by stanza — was all fin-
ished before it first saw the light in 1807. In form it is ir-
regular and original. And perhaps the most remarkable thing
in its structure is the frequent change of the keynote, and the
skill and delicacy with which the transitions are made. "The
feet throughout are iambic. The lines vary in length from the
Alexandrine to the line with two accents. There is a constant
ebb and flow in the full tide of song, but scarce two waves
are alike." (Hawes Turner, *Selections from Wordsworth.*)

In the "notes" to the *Selections* just referred to, there is
an excellent commentary on this *Ode on Immortality*, almost
every line of which is worthy of minute analysis and study.
Several of the following are suggested by Mr. Turner.

(1.)   *The winds come to me, from the fields of sleep,*
The morning breeze blowing from the fields that were dark
during the hours of sleep.

(2.)   *But there's a tree, of many, one,*
Compare Browning's *May and Death :*

Only one little sight, one plant
Woods have in May, &c.

(3.)   *The pansy at my feet*
    Doth the same tale repeat,

French " Pensée." " Pansies, that's for thoughts." Ophelia in *Hamlet.*

(4.)   *Our birth is but a sleep and a forgetting,*

This thought Wordsworth owed, consciously or unconsciously, to Plato. Though he tells us in the Fenwick note that he did not mean to *inculcate* the belief, there is no doubt that he clung to the notion of a life pre-existing the present, on grounds similar to those on which he believed in a life to come. But there are some differences in the way in which the idea commended itself to Plato and to Wordsworth. The stress was laid by Wordsworth on the effect of terrestrial life in putting the higher faculties to sleep, and making us "forget the glories we have known." Plato, on the other hand, looked upon the mingled experiences of mundane life as inducing a gradual but slow remembrance of the past. Compare Tennyson's *Two Voices,* and Wordsworth's sonnet :

" Man's life is like a sparrow, mighty king."

(5.)   *Filling from time to time his "humorous stage"*
        With all the persons,

i. e. with the *dramatis personæ.*

(6.)   *Thou eye among the blind,*
        That, deaf and silent, read'st the eternal deep,

There is an admirable parallel illustration of Wordsworth's use of this figure (describing one sense in terms of another), in the lines in *Aira Force Valley :*

" A soft eye-music of slow waving boughs."

(7.)   *Full soon thy Soul shall have her earthly freight,*
        And custom lie upon thee with a weight,
        Heavy as frost, and deep almost as life!

Compare with this the lines in the fourth book of *The Ex-cursion,* beginning:

> Alas! the endowment of immortal Pain
> Is matched unequally with custom, time.

(8.)   *Fallings from us, vanishings,*

The outward sensible universe, visible and tangible, seeming to fall away from us, as unreal, to vanish in unsubstantiality. See the explanation of this youthful experience in the Fenwick note. That confession of his boyish days at Hawkshead, "many times, while going to school, have I grasped at a wall or tree, to recall myself from this abyss of idealism to the reality" (by which he explains those

> fallings from us, vanishings, &c.),

suggests a similar experience and confession of Cardinal Newman's in his *Apologia* (See p. 67).

The Rev. Robert Perceval Graves, late of Windermere, now of Dublin, wrote thus in 1850: "I remember Mr. Wordsworth saying that, at a particular stage of his mental progress, he used to be frequently so rapt into an unreal transcendental world of ideas that the external world seemed no longer to exist in relation to him, and he had to reconvince himself of its existence by *clasping a tree,* or something that happened to be near him. I could not help connecting this fact with that obscure passage in his great Ode on the 'Intimations of Immortality,' in which he speaks of

> Those obstinate questionings
> Of sense and outward things,
> Fallings from us, vanishings. "

Professor Bonamy Price farther confirms the explanation

which Wordsworth gave of the passage, in an account of a
conversation he had with the poet. It was an experience, however, not, I think, as Mr. Price imagines, peculiar
to Wordsworth — and its value would be much lessened if it
were so — but one to which (as the poet said to Miss Fenwick) "every one, if he would look back, could bear testimony."

"OXFORD, *April* 21, 1881.

"MY DEAR SIR, — You will be glad, I am sure, to receive
an interpretation, which chance enabled me to obtain from
Wordsworth himself, of a passage in the immortal Ode to Immortality. . . .

"It happened one day that the poet, my wife, and I were
taking a walk together by the side of Rydal Water. We were
then by the sycamores under Nab Scar. The aged poet was
in a most genial mood, and it suddenly occurred to me that
I might, without unwarrantable presumption, seize the golden
opportunity thus offered, and ask him to explain these mys-
terious words. So I addressed him with an apology, and
begged him to explain, what my own feeble mother-wit was
unable to unravel, and for which I had in vain sought the
assistance of others, what were those "fallings from us, vanishings," for which, above all other things, he gave God
thanks. The venerable old man raised his aged form erect ;
he was walking in the middle, and passed across me to a five-
barred gate in the wall which bounded the road on the side
of the lake. He clenched the top bar firmly with his right
hand, pushed strongly against it, and then uttered these ever-
memorable words: 'There was a time in my life when I had
to push against something that resisted, to be sure that there
was anything outside of me. I was sure of my own mind ;

everything else fell away, and vanished into thought.' Thought, he was sure of; matter, for him, at the moment, was an un-reality — nothing but a thought. Such natural spontaneous idealism has probably never been felt by any other man.

BONAMY PRICE."

Professor Knight.

The following is from S. T. Coleridge's *Biographia Liter-aria* (ch. xxii., p. 229, ed. 1817).

" To the ' Ode on the Intimations of Immortality from Rec-ollections of Early Childhood,' the poet might have prefixed the lines which Dante addresses to one of his own Canzoni:

> ' Canzone, i' credo, che saranno radi
> Color che tua ragione intendan bene :
> Tanto lor sei faticoso ed alto.'

> ' O lyric song, there will be few, think I,
> Who may thy import understand aright :
> Thou art for them so arduous and so high ! '

But the Ode was intended for such readers only as had been accustomed to watch the flux and reflux of their inmost na-ture, to venture at times into the twilight realms of conscious-ness, and to feel a deep interest in modes of inmost being, to which they know that the attributes of time and space are inapplicable and alien, but which yet cannot be conveyed, save in symbols of time and space. For such readers the sense is sufficiently plain, and they will be as little disposed to charge Mr. Wordsworth with believing the Platonic pre-existence, in the ordinary interpretation of the words, as I am to believe that Plato himself ever meant or taught it."

CPSIA information can be obtained
at www.ICGtesting.com
Printed in the USA
LVHW040800020223
738373LV00021B/19

9 781168 709851